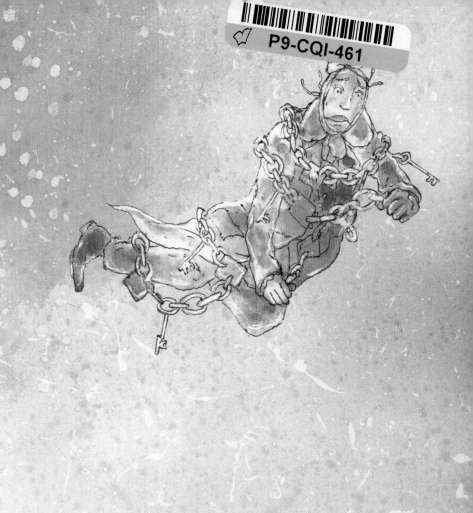

A Christmas Carol

Illustrated by Alan Marks

Retold by Lesley Sims

Based on a story by Charles Dickens

Once upon a Christmas Eve,
Scrooge was counting money.

Ebenezer Scrooge!

A greedy,

grasping,

gruesome old man...

...so cold inside, his face looked frozen.

He cared for no one
and, now his old friend Marley was dead,
no one cared for him.

His clerk, Bob Cratchit,
shivered in their icy office.

"Might we light a fire, sir?"
"Certainly not!" said Scrooge.

Two gentlemen came by,
collecting for the poor.

"Let them starve!" Scrooge sneered.

Then a red-nosed carol singer
tried his luck.

"Be off with you!" snapped Scrooge.

"Merry Christmas," said Bob Cratchit,
as they left that night.

"Bah, humbug!" said Scrooge.

Scrooge was heading for bed, when every bell in his house started to ring...

CLANG! CLANG!

"Who's there?"
Scrooge asked,
in a quavery voice.

Scrooge... came the ghostly reply.
Scrooge...

"Marley?" said Scrooge.
"Is that you?"

Change your ways or pay the consequences,

warned Marley's ghost.

I cared only for money, moaned Marley.

Now money and misery are my only company.
Clanking chains and cash boxes for all eternity...

With a dreadful wail of torment,
Marley turned to go.

"Wait!" Scrooge cried.
"What has this to do with me?"

Tonight, you will be visited by three ghosts.
Listen to them and you may save yourself.

"What nonsense!" said Scrooge.

On the stroke of one,
  Scrooge woke to see a spirit staring at him.

    "Wh-who are you?" Scrooge
    stuttered, through chattering teeth.

I am the Ghost of Christmas Past.
  Rise and walk with me...

They floated to a deserted schoolroom,
where a lonely boy sat, hunched in gloom.

"That poor boy is me!" murmured Scrooge, in surprise.
"Oh, I wish I had given the carol singer something..."

With a whirl and a twirl, they were off to a dance.

"It's my old boss, Fezziwig!
He knew how to throw a
Christmas party," cried Scrooge.

And was that Scrooge's sweetheart,
from so many years ago?

"I cannot marry you,"
she wept. "Ebenezer,
you only love money."

"No more memories!" shouted Scrooge
and he slammed down the ghost's hat, hard, on his head.

The ghost sank into the floorboards with a sigh.

The clock struck again and a second ghost appeared.

Merry Christmas Scrooge!

I am the Ghost of
Christmas Present.

Celebrate with me!

Scrooge and the spirit soared through the air,
seeing Christmas joy wherever they went.

It lit up the night like stars in the sky.

In grand houses all around town,
people were eating, drinking
and making merry.

Even the Cratchits, with a simple meal for their
Christmas feast, were full of cheer.

"God bless us every one!"
said Tiny Tim, the youngest.

"He looks pale," thought Scrooge. "Is he ill?"
The spirit's response echoed in his head.

If things go on as they are, he won't see another Christmas.

Somewhere, a clock chimed and the spirit faded away.
As Scrooge shivered in darkness,

he saw a hooded phantom coming closer.

"Are you the Ghost of Christmas
Yet To Come?" asked Scrooge.

The phantom said nothing,
but pointed a bony finger.

A group of men were talking about... someone.

"He's dead and good riddance!"

"No one will miss him."

"No one liked him."

"Who is this man?" Scrooge asked.
"This unfortunate, unmourned soul?"

The spirit stayed silent,
his bony hand pointing to a gravestone.

Trembling, Scrooge read
the name engraved upon it...

...and looked at the spirit in horror.

"No!" he begged.
"Don't let me die. I can change.

I *will* change."

EBENEZER
SCROOGE

He ran to clutch the spirit's arm and it turned into his bedpost.

"I'm alive!" he shouted,
leaping for joy. "Alive!"

Scrooge raced to his window.

What's today, boy?

Christmas Day of course!

"Buy me the biggest goose you can find,"
Scrooge ordered. "And hurry!"

The boy was soon back. Scrooge chuckled with glee.
"I'll send it to the Cratchits. What a surprise they'll have."

Everyone had a surprise, for Scrooge *did* change.

What was more, from that day on,
he kept Christmas in his heart, all year round.

Lovely day, Ebenezer! Hello, Tim.

A lovely day, indeed!

Edited by Jenny Tyler

Designed by Louise Flutter

First published in 2007 by Usborne Publishing Ltd, 83-85 Saffron Hill, London EC1N 8RT, England.
www.usborne.com Copyright © 2007 Usborne Publishing Ltd. The name Usborne and the devices ♀ ⊕ are Trade Marks
of Usborne Publishing Ltd. All rights reserved. No part of this publication may be reproduced, stored in a retrieval system,
or transmitted in any form or by any means, electronic, mechanical, photocopying, recording or otherwise,
without the prior permission of the publisher. First published in America in 2007. UE. Printed in Dubai.